Celebrating your year

1955

a very special year for

First printed in 2020 in the USA (ISBN 979-8684074448).
Revised in 2021, 2nd Edition (ISBN 978-0-6450623-2-8).
Self-published through Kindle Direct Publishing and
IngramSpark for Kid Hero Stories Pte. Ltd.

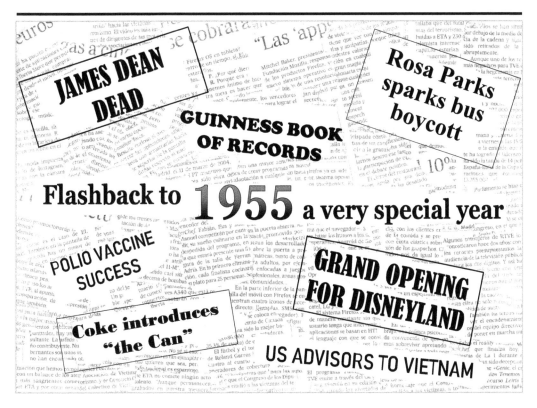

JAMES DEAN DEAD

Rosa Parks sparks bus boycott

GUINNESS BOOK OF RECORDS

Flashback to **1955** a very special year

POLIO VACCINE SUCCESS

GRAND OPENING FOR DISNEYLAND

Coke introduces "the Can"

US ADVISORS TO VIETNAM

Let's flashback to 1955, a very special year.

Was this the year you were born?

Was this the year you were married?

Whatever the reason, this book is a celebration of your year,

THE YEAR 1955.

Turn the pages to discover a book packed with fun-filled fabulous facts. We look at the people, the places, the politics and the pleasures that made 1955 unique and helped shape the world we know today.

So get your time-travel suit on, and enjoy this trip down memory lane, to rediscover what life was like, back in the year 1955.

Ice—Ice—All the ice you want without your lifting a finger! No trays to fill, spill, empty or forget to refill. That's what *this* Servel Gas refrigerator gives you—an icemaker that's as automatic as your desire for a cool drink—plus automatic defrosting. And that isn't all! From the freezer to the food compartment, everything stays at precisely the right temperature in a Gas refrigerator—noiselessly, silently—with no whir, no shut-off and bang-on. In fact, there are no moving parts to wear; that's why Gas refrigerators are guaranteed 10 years—twice as long as any other refrigerator. See them at your Gas company or Gas appliance dealer's now!   American Gas Association.

Gas—the modern fuel for <u>automatic</u> cooking... refrigeration... water-heating... house-heating... air-conditioning... clothes-drying... incineration.

Contents

Family Life in 1955 America

Imagine if time-travel was a reality, and one fine morning you wake up to find yourself flashed back in time, back to the year 1955.

What would life be like for a typical family, in a typical town, somewhere in America?

A typical family in 1955.

The post-war boom delivered us a booming economy, booming birth numbers, booming suburbs, and the booming trappings of the consumerist culture we still live in today.

Our rising middle classes were feeling an pressing need to spend, with consumer demand for everything innovative, bigger, or better, reaching new highs year after year.

In the year 1955 there were 4.05 million babies born (up from 2.8 million at the end of the war ten years earlier).[1]

Massive suburban developments, built on the outskirts of towns, catered to our increased demand for family homes. Sales were boosted by returned soldiers who had access to low interest loans through the G.I. Bill of 1944.

From 1952-1958, 17,300 homes were built in the massive suburban development of Levittown, Pennsylvania.

Our middle-class desire for everything new and modern, which we just loved to show-off, kept businesses profitable and production on the increase. With only 6% of the world's population in 1955, the USA was producing almost half the world's goods.

An energetic advertising industry, through TV, radio and print, ensured we always knew what our next purchase could and should be.

[1] https://247wallst.com/special-report/2017/04/10/how-many-people-were-born-the-year-you-were-born/5/.
[2] ageofaffluence.weebly.com.

Joining the television in our families' list of must-haves were: defrost refrigerators, front-loading dryers, fully-automatic washing machines, vacuum cleaners, air-conditioning and heating units, milkshake makers, and a multitude of other kitchen gadgets and home appliances. In addition we needed a family car, motorcycle, bicycles, hiking, camping, picnic gear, and much, much more.

New! G·E automatic cooking unit
You just "set it and forget it"

The median family income was $3,400 a year,[1] unemployment was 4.2% and falling, with GDP at 7.1%.[2]

Average costs in 1955 [3]	
New house	$10,950
New car	$1,900
Television	$100
A gallon of gas	$0.23

But beneath the appearance of domestic bliss, Americans were deeply concerned. The threat of the Soviet Union (USSR) was ever present. The Cold War dominated US policies and communist fears gripped the nation throughout the decade and beyond.

By the end of 1955, both the US and USSR had successfully developed and detonated hydrogen bombs. The nuclear arms race was well underway. We would endure another 35 years of tension between the two super-powers before the Cold War finally ended with the dissolution of the Soviet Union in 1991.

[1] census.gov/library/publications.html.
[2] thebalance.com/unemployment-rate-by-year-3305506 and thebalance.com/us-gdp-by-year-3305543.
[3] thepeoplehistory.com.

new Maytag can save 9 gallons of <u>hot</u> water per load!

AUTOMATIC WATER LEVEL CONTROL—
Saves up to 11½ gallons of water on
small loads. 9 gallons are hot water!

FASTEST SAFETY BRAKE—Maytag Safety
Lid stops action the moment it's opened.
Sure protection for your youngsters.

It's <u>completely</u> automatic, even for small loads!

Save $11^1/_2$ gallons of water every time you wash a small load–and 9 gallons of this is *hot* water! Think of the savings over the years. Exclusive new Automatic Water Level Control saves on *both* wash and rinse, uses only the water you need for any size load! On full loads the Maytag Automatic uses less water than any other agitator type automatic–as much as 50% less. Exclusive Gyrafoam action and Double-Spin Tubs wash the grimiest work clothes–the most delicate fabrics–thoroughly clean. Matching gas or electric dryer. Ask your dealer how *easy* it is to own a Maytag. *The Maytag Company, Newton, Iowa.*

Fastest safety brake–Maytag Safety Lid stops action the moment it's opened. Sure protection for your youngsters.

A Decade of Change for the United Kingdom

Now just imagine you flashed back to a town
in 1955 United Kingdom or Western Europe.

Unlike boom-time America, a very different
picture would await you.

Many major cities like London bore the brunt of destruction from
WWII bombings. The rebuilding process had required major loans
from the USA and other nations, leaving the UK heavily in long-term
debt. Post-war Brits were forced to tighten their collective belts,
through austerity measures on everything from fabrics to food.

A central London street in 1955.

With the last of the post-war austerity restrictions ending in 1954, the
British populace was feeling the positive winds of change. Job security
and record low unemployment saw the middle and working classes
feeling prosperous and optimistic. Living standards were rising and
families had money to spend.

Young adults in particular had spare cash to burn on leisure and luxuries. Even teenagers had money to spend. Looking for a new voice, the British youth of the mid 50s turned to American rock-and-roll music and fashion, giving rise to a distinct youth culture focused on freedom and rebellion.

British teenagers at a party.

Internationally, lack of excess finance made it increasingly difficult for Great Britain to continue financing and keeping secure its far-flung colonies. As a result, many British colonies would be released in the following 10 years, gaining independence as new nations. The United Kingdom was losing its super-power status on the world's stage.

It's an eye-filling picture, and you can't mistake it.

From up front, from the rear, or simply sitting curbside, this long, lithe styling is a fresh new grace that says "1955 Buick" and nothing but.

Sure is a honey, you say–*wonder what goes with it?*

In one brief phrase–thrills a-plenty.

Walloping new power, for one thing–record-high power from great new V8 engines of constantly advanced design. 236 hp in the Roadmaster, Super and Century–188 hp in the low-price Special–*and all with better gas mileage to boot.*

But the biggest thrill, we believe, will come when you try today's Dynaflow Drive.

To the power blades inside this wondrously smooth transmission, Buick engineers have brought the principle of the modern plane's "variable pitch propeller."

You use one pitch of the blades for new gas-saving economy in your normal driving and cruising. You switch the pitch for spectacular performance merely by pressing the pedal to the floor.

Instantly, irresistibly, off you go in a sweep of infinitely smooth power delivery–with solid new getaway, or an electrifying new safety-surge for sudden acceleration when you need it–a response thrilling beyond words.

Drop in on us this week and try the new Buick. It's the *only* way to know what a superb thriller–and a great buy–this new automobile really is.

First it warms your heart... (That Thunderbird styling!)

Then it reads your mind...(That Trigger-Torque Power!)

It's amazing how just *looking* at the '55 Ford gives so many people that wonderful feeling. Why not? There's "Thunderbird" written in almost every line... from the hooded headlights to the flat rear deck. Inside, you'll see new exciting color harmonies in durable fabrics. All in all, there isn't a more *pleasing* car in sight.

Behind the wheel of the new Ford, *you* become a new man. For under your foot lies response so eager and alive, you almost believe it's clairvoyant! This is Ford's Trigger-Torque power... and it replies to your driving demands with split-second agility. There's safety in power like this... to whizz you out of traffic snarls... and to pass you ahead when passing is called for. Three new stout-hearted engines to choose from. And at least a score of other new engineering features. Reading about it is nowhere near the fun of driving the new Ford. So why not visit your dealer today?

Our Love Affair with Cars

By 1955, the US dominated the world's car market, producing more than half of all new vehicles. In just ten years, the car industry had shifted from fabricating utilitarian war tanks and trucks, to producing fashionable consumer vehicles, the kind of which we just had to have.

There were now 52 million registered cars on US roads, up from 25 million ten years earlier.[1] Rising incomes meant the car was no longer considered a luxury reserved only for the wealthy. Our love affair with cars had begun.

General Motors rolls out the cars at its new engine plant in Flint, MI.

Teenagers at a drive-through in the mid-50s.

Services related business such as drive-through restaurants and drive-in cinemas were springing up everywhere, especially popular among the younger generation.

[1] fhwa.dot.gov/ohim/summary95/mv200.pdf.

Our love affair with cars grew hand-in-hand with the post-war baby boom and housing construction boom. Where would we be without our cars? How else could we get from our far-flung suburban homes to our downtown offices?

The newest of the new!

Advanced '55 Studebaker

NEW VISIBILITY! NEW COLOR! NEW POWER! NO INCREASE IN PRICES!

Car manufacturers competed for our attention with stylish designs, larger engines, and added detailing. The rising middle classes had money to spend, and cars became the ultimate status symbol.

Cars were no longer just a necessity; they had become an expression of our personality. Sturdy, sporty, powerful or luxurious, cars now came in a wide range of styles, colors, and price-points. Decorative chrome and tail fins reached new heights as the decade progressed, adorned with wings and stripes for added pizzazz.

FOR FUTURE STYLING AND SUPER POWER IT PAYS TO OWN A NEW 1955 MERCURY

MERCURY DIVISION • FORD MOTOR COMPANY

Five car-producing countries dominated the industry by the start of 1955: England, France, Germany and Italy, with America in the top spot. (Japan had yet to enter this elite group.)

Top: MGA by MG, 1955-56.
Left: SAAB 93, 1955.
Below: Pegaso Z-103, 1955.

American car manufacturers produced 8 million vehicles in 1955 alone, accounting for more than 90% of cars sold in the country and more than half of the cars sold internationally.

Detroit was America's car manufacturing powerhouse, where "the Big Three" (General Motors, Ford and Chrysler) produced year-on-year bigger, longer and heavier gas-guzzlers to satisfy the 50s consumer desire for power and style over efficiency and safety.

By the end of the decade Detroit would become the 4th largest city in the US. A whopping one in six American adults would be employed in the car industry nation-wide.[1]

GM Chevrolet assembly line, 1955.

In 1955, General Motors sold more than all its competitors combined, becoming the first US company to generate more than $1 billion in sales.[2]

[1] theweek.com/articles/461968/rise-fall-detroit-timeline.
[2] ageofaffluence.weebly.com.

"Guests of Honor" Wherever They Go!

Not long after a motorist takes delivery of his first Cadillac car, he makes a truly wonderful and thrilling discovery.

No matter where he travels at the wheel of his Cadillac, he finds that he is accorded an extra measure of courtesy and respect.

And this discovery will be all the more rewarding for the man or woman who makes the move to Cadillac in 1955. For the "car of cars" now offers more of everything to inspire the respect and admiration of people everywhere.

Its world-famous beauty, for example, is more majestic and distinctive than ever before. Its celebrated interior luxury and elegance are far more wonderful to behold... and to enjoy. And its performance is, from every standpoint, the finest in Cadillac history!

If you haven't as yet taken the time for a personal inspection and demonstration of the 1955 Cadillac—you ought to come in soon and do so.

You'll be a most welcome guest—at any time!

BIGGER-THAN-LIFE! THAT'S THE GIANT PICTURE YOU GET WITH THE NEW 24-INCH "BAYLOR". EBONY FINISH. MODEL 24S512, $299.95.

The big new television thrill from RCA Victor—

BIGGER-THAN-LIFE 24-INCH TV WITH THE "ALL-CLEAR" PICTURE

TV entertainment has come of age . . . with today's bigger, more spectacular programs. But you miss half the fun of a king-size show when it's squeezed into a small-size screen.

That's why the new and beautiful RCA Victor 24-inch table models make such happy news. For only $299.95— less than you might pay for many a smaller-screen set— you can now have a picture that's actually bigger-than-life!

What's more, RCA Victor TV sets are the only ones with the famous "All-Clear" Picture—and that's all-important with 24-inch TV. You see, as the picture grows bigger, fine picture quality becomes increasingly necessary. The RCA Victor "All-Clear" Picture—with 212% greater contrast— is TV's finest and clearest. It's another RCA Victor exclusive!

All RCA Victor 24-inch sets also have such advances as "Golden Throat" Fidelity Sound . . . "Magic Monitor" chassis for finest reception possible . . . new light-up tuning. See the great variety of handsome RCA Victor table models and consoles now on display at your RCA Victor dealer's. See for yourself why every year more people buy RCA Victor than any other television.

Enter the Kraft Parkay Margarine Color TV Contest. 45 RCA Victor 21-in. Color TV sets as first prizes. Get details from your RCA Victor dealer or your grocer.

Top value—peak performance—at every price level—$149.95 to $500

Suggested VHF list prices shown, subject to change without notice. Slightly higher is for West and South. UHF optional at extra cost. RCA Factory Service is available in most TV areas, but only to RCA Victor TV owners. Ask your dealer.

212% GREATER PICTURE CONTRAST—by actual scientific measurement—in RCA Victor's famous "All-Clear" aluminized picture tube. A sharp, clear picture like this is all-important in bigger-than-life 24-inch TV...and RCA Victor brings it to you.

TV entertainment has come of age... with today's bigger, more spectacular programs. But you miss half the fun of a king-size show when it's squeezed into a small-size screen.

That's why the new and beautiful RCA Victor 24-inch table models make such happy news. For only $299.95–less than you might pay for many a smaller-screen set–you can now have a picture that's actually bigger-than-life!

What's more, RCA Victor TV sets are the only ones with the famous "All-Clear" Picture–and that's all-important with 24-inch TV. You see, as the picture grows bigger, fine picture quality becomes increasingly necessary. The RCA Victor "All-Clear" Picture–with 212% greater contrast–is TV's finest and clearest. It's another RCA Victor exclusive!

All RCA Victor 24-inch sets also have such advances as "Golden Throat" Fidelity Sound... "Magic Monitor" chassis for finest reception possible... new light-up tuning. See the great variety of handsome RCA Victor table models and consoles now on display at your RCA Victor dealer's. See for yourself why every year more people buy RCA Victor than any other television.

212% greater picture contrast–by actual scientific measurement–in RCA Victor's famous "All-Clear" *aluminized* picture tube. A sharp, clear picture like this is all-important in bigger-than-life 24-inch TV... and RCA Victor brings it to you.

Tuning in to Television

Typical family watching television in the 50s.

By 1955, 64% of US households owned a television set.[1] Television had firmly become the preferred means of entertainment for our rising middle classes.

The early 50s would become known as the first "Golden Age of Television". During this time, live TV broadcasts from New York City dominated, based on radio and the theatrical traditions of Broadway.

However by 1955, the newer formats produced out of Los Angeles were gaining in popularity–sitcoms, soap operas, westerns, quiz shows, crime and medical dramas would soon become our primetime staples.

Natalie Wood and Gig Young in *Warner Brothers Presents* (ABC. 1955-1956).

The big Hollywood film studios, who had until now frowned upon television, had finally accepted that TV was here to stay, and they sought profitable ways to enter the small-screen business.

In 1955, Warner Brothers, MGM and 20th Century Fox aired their first made-for-TV shows. Over the next five years these Hollywood produced programs would succeed in dominating TV primetime.

[1] americancentury.omeka.wlu.edu/items/show/136.

Most Popular TV Shows of 1955

1	The $64,000 Question	11	General Electric Theater
2	I Love Lucy	12	Private Secretary
3	The Ed Sullivan Show	=	Ford Theater
4	Disneyland	14	The Red Skelton Show
5	The Jack Benny Show	15	The George Gobel Show
6	December Bride	16	Arthur Godfrey's Talent Scouts
7	You Bet Your Life	17	The Lineup
8	Dragnet	18	The Perry Como Show
9	The Millionaire	19	The Honeymooners
10	I've Got a Secret	20	The Adventures of Robin Hood

* From the Nielsen Media Research 1955-56 season of top-rated primetime television series.

The $64,000 Question captured the nation's attention from the moment it debuted in June 1955, till its sudden demise 3 years later. The show was canceled following the scandalous exposure of game show rigging, where questions and answers were provided to preferred contestants prior to filming. (CBS. 1955-1958).

Ronald Regan, as host and part owner of *General Electric Theater*, became known as "The Great Communicator". It is said he developed his public-speaking skills through the many public forums he was invited to speak at. (CBS. 1953-1962).

THEATER
RONALD REAGAN

Angie Dickinson and James Craig in
The Millionaire (CBS. 1955-1960).

The original Mouseketeers of
The Mickey Mouse Club (ABC. 1955-59).

The television networks were quick to turn out new programs to keep us tuning in. Here are just a few of the new programs that aired for the first time in 1955: *The Millionaire, The Mickey Mouse Club, The Benny Hill Show* (UK), and *The Adventures of Robin Hood (UK)*. Other notables include *The $64,000 Question, The Perry Como Show, The Honeymooners, This is Your Life* (UK) and the hugely popular *Gunsmoke,* which aired for 20 seasons.

James Arness, Amanda Blake, Milburn Stone, & Dennis Weaver in *Gunsmoke* (CBS. 1955-1975).

Alexander Gauge & Richard Greene in *The Adventures of Robin Hood* (ITV. 1955-1959).

PACKAGED PRODUCE HELPS ME SHOP IN A JIFFY

"I never have to wait till a clerk is free! Fruits and vegetables are weighed  and priced , packaged in Cellophane ... I just pick what I want and go on my way! They're cleaner, too ...ready to pop into the refrigerator, wrapper and all. And many are trimmed to save work and waste."

DU PONT
Cellophane

DUPONT

BETTER THINGS FOR BETTER LIVING
... THROUGH CHEMISTRY

Look at "Cavalcade of America" on Television

Shopping's easier: fruits and vegetables are clean and fresh in DuPont Cellophane

What is it about McDonalds that makes the fast-food giant so extraordinary? It remains one of the world's most loved fast-food chains, with almost 40,000 restaurants in more than 100 countries. But it all started back in 1955, with the vision of one man–Ray Kroc.

McDonalds was created in 1948 when brothers Dick and Mac McDonald opened their first self-service restaurant in San Bernardino, California. By eliminating waiters, focusing on a minimal, highly profitable burger-focussed menu, and developing assembly-line food systems, the brothers "invented" the notion of fast-food.

Dick and Mac McDonalds' first burger restaurant in San Bernardino, 1948.

Ray Kroc's first McDonalds franchise opened in Illinois, Chicago on 15th April 1955.

Enter Ray Kroc, seller of milkshake machines. Kroc had come to see why McDonalds had purchased so many of his machines. Impressed by their operations, Kroc convinced the brothers to give him nation-wide franchise rights.

In return for half a percent of gross sales, Kroc would seek funding, set up the franchisees, and absorb all risks. Business savvy Kroc separately set up another company, to buy the land and build the restaurants that all franchisees would be required to lease.

To gain total control, Kroc bought out the McDonald brothers' share in 1961 for $2.7 million, and the rest, as they say, is history.

The new Underwood 150 is the typewriter
designed to keep your hands lovely to look at.

Two important improvements make the new Underwood 150 the typewriter most wanted by the girls who make business hum. Underwood has always been designed with the user in mind. That's why it's so good looking and has so many extra features to make turning out crisp, clean work practically automatic. Now, look how Underwood and Underwood alone helps you keep fingernails and hands lovely to look at, lovely to touch!

Exclusive half-moon keys: formed to fit fingers. Half-moon tops mean fingernails never touch the keys. No more worrying about short unfashionable fingernails, chipped nail polish! Exclusive touch tuning: Stubborn typewriter keys often give girls rough, widened fingertips. Underwood's touch is kitten-soft. 28 easy-to-set touch variations! You choose touch to suit finger-tips, always look fresh from the manicurist!

Rosa Parks and the Montgomery Bus Boycott

42-year-old civil rights activist Rosa Parks was arrested on a Montgomery bus on 1st December 1955, for refusing to give up her seat to a white passenger.

During Park's trial 4 days later, 500 supporters came to the court-house, while a further 40,000 commuters boycotted the buses, car pooling or walking to work.

Led by a young Dr. Martin Luther King Jr., the Montgomery Bus Boycott followed, lasting 381 days until a U.S Supreme Court ruling declared segregation on public transport to be unconstitutional.

Left, top to bottom: Rosa Parks with Dr. Martin Luther King jr. 1955.
Riding a bus, 1956.
Being fingerprinted by police, 1956.

The No. 2857 bus on which Parks was riding before her arrest, exhibited at the Henry Ford Museum in Detroit MI. Statues of Parks' sitting on a bus at the National Civil Rights Museum in Memphis TN, and in the United States Capitol.

Parks continued fighting for equality throughout her long and prolific life.

When she died on the 24th October 2005, she became the first woman, and only second African American, to lie in honor in the US State Rotunda.

The Cold War–Nuclear Arms Race

Cold War tensions between the two former allies–the USSR and the USA–continued from post war 1945 till 1991.

Starting in the USA as policies for communist containment, the distrust and misunderstanding between the two sides quickly escalated from political squabbling to a military nuclear arms race. Trillions of dollars in military spending saw both sides stockpile their nuclear arsenals, strategically pointing and positioning their missiles closer and closer to each other.

The superpowers also raced to develop more powerful bombs and longer reaching missiles. The USA tested its first hydrogen bomb in 1954, with the USSR testing theirs in November 1955.

In January 1955, the US Airforce awarded Convair a contract to develop a long range intercontinental ballistic missile, capable of delivering a nuclear weapon. Two years later the Soviets would confirm they had long range missiles able to reach any corner of the earth.

By 1955, the USA had a stockpile of 2422 nuclear weapons, against the Soviet's 200 weapons.[1] Both sides continued to increase their stockpiles. American stockpiles peaked in 1966 with a total of 31,175 against the Soviet's 7,089 weapons.[1]

The USSR continued to grow their stockpile until 1988, after which the two superpowers ended the Cold War in 1991, with the signing of a denuclearization treaty.

USA ballistic missile ready to launch, 1955.

[1] tandfonline.com/doi/pdf/10.2968/066004008.

The Cold War–On the Ground and in the Skies

14th May– The Soviet Union and seven Eastern Bloc allies signed *The Warsaw Pact*, cementing the communist military and political alliance as a counter to NATO.

Fearful that a "domino effect" would see an uncontained spread of communism across the world, the 1950s saw America embroiled in two major Southeast Asian wars–the Korean War (1950-1953) and the Vietnam War (1955-1973).

On the 1st November 1955, US personnel of the Military Assistance Advisory Group were deployed to train the South Vietnamese Army. This would mark the start of US involvement in the Vietnamese war.

The US committed to supporting South Vietnam, financially and militarily, during its 30-year-long bloody civil war against North Vietnam (the Viet Cong). At the same time, communist China and USSR were jointly aiding the Viet Cong's invasion southward. Vietnam had become a Cold War battlefield.

The Cold War turned skywards on 29th July 1955, when the USA announced its intent to launch an artificial satellite. Four days later, on 2nd August, the Soviets announced their intention to do the same "in the near future." Space would become the next battlefield for superpower superiority. The Space Race, which was to dominate most of the 1960s, was underway.

The Man
in the $70,000 hat

He's Navy... every inch. A flier in the New Air Navy. Young... dedicated... serious. A man whose business is the active defense of every American.

Maybe you know him. He comes from the house next door... or the farm down the road. Yesterday he delivered your newspaper, or lent a hand at harvest time. Today he's flying jets from a Navy carrier.

He's a proud man... and he has a right to be. Not everybody can be a Navy flier. Not everybody can graduate to wear glistening wings of gold and the stripes of a Navy ensign.

Training is thorough... painstaking and unforgettable. It's executive training that will stand him in good stead all his life.

Private money can't buy it. But the Navy gives it to those who qualify. It costs about $70,000 to build a Navy flier... and when a man graduates... he's ready to wear that $70,000 hat.

He's equipped to man the newest Navy jets. He's learned to live by Navy's strict code of safety... both in aircraft and on the ground. He's an Air Navy man... and America is proud of him.

America needs more men like him now!

Men who can carry responsibility... who want to take their place in the new jet age. Men who want to take hold of their future and give it direction. Men who can wear a $70,000 hat. Men like yourself, perhaps?

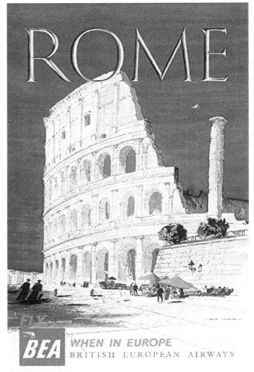

British Vintage Airline Posters from 1955.

EXTRA!   *The Daily* PRINCETONIAN   **EXTRA!**

Vol. LXXIX, No. 51   THE DAILY PRINCETONIAN, MONDAY, APRIL 18, 1955   Entered as Second-Class Matter Post Office, Princeton, N. J.   FIVE CENTS

EINSTEIN DIES!

Oppenheimer Pays Tribute to Friend

BY ROBERT D. HOLGARD '57 and EBERHARD FABER '57

Public officials, friends and colleagues throughout the nation mourned the loss of the teacher, scholar and world-renowned nuclear physicist today following the news of Dr. Einstein's death.

Dr. J. Robert Oppenheimer, director of the Princeton Institute for Advanced Study, where Einstein has carried on his work since 1933, when he came to America as a voluntary exile from Germany, stated that "the death of Albert Einstein is a kind of mourning for all scientists and for most men. He was one of the great of all ages."

Dr. John Von Neumann, member of the Atomic Energy Commission and professor at the Institute, expressed the belief that "Dr. Einstein has left an indelible mark upon contemporary physics and the philosophy of science. At least two generations of physicists have been profoundly influenced by his methods," he said.

Dodds Cites Human Sympathy

Dr. Harold W. Dodds told the Princetonian this morning that "the contributions which Dr. Einstein made to man's understanding of nature are beyond assessment in our day. Only future generations will be competent to grasp their full significance.

"He combined broad human sympathy and a deep appreciation of the arts with his scientific genius," Dr.

Dr. Albert Einstein (1879-1955)

Academic Freedom Was A Concern Of Physicist

Scientist, 76, Succumbs Here After Brief Hospital Illness

Eisenhower Praises Character, Work Of German-Born Relativity Theorist

By RAYMOND W. APPLE JR. '57

Dr. Albert Einstein died this morning at Princeton Hospital. Seventy-six last month, the physicist succumbed at 1:15 a.m. today to heart disease.

He was admitted to the hospital last Friday after a two-day illness, according to Dr. Guy K. Dean, his personal physician. He had apparently been making a recovery from a leak in the aorta and gall bladder complications.

Best known for his theory of special relativity—first published in 1905—Einstein appears certain to be accorded a historic place in man's quest for scientific achievement beside the names of Archimedes, Euclid, Galileo, Copernicus and Sir Isaac Newton.

In Washington, President Eisenhower issued the following statement: "For 22 years the United States has been the freely-chosen home of Albert Einstein. For 15 years he has been a citizen of the United States by his own free and deliberate choice. Americans welcomed him here. Americans were proud, too, that he sought and found here a climate of freedom in his search for knowledge and truth.

"No other man contributed so much to the vast expansion of twentieth-century knowledge, yet no other man was more modest in the posses-

mighty creative ability of the individual in a free society."

Dr. Thomas S. Harvey, the Hospital's pathologist, performed an autopsy shortly before noon today and concurred with Dr. Dean's diagnosis.

"A small leak from the aneurysmal sac into the tissues behind the aorta brought death," Dr. Dean said. Dr. Harvey explained that Dr. Einstein's aorta (the main blood vessel in the body) was "bulged out like an old inner tube and finally broke." He added that the ailment was similar to arterio-sclerosis, or hardening of the arteries.

A Professor Emeritus in the School of Mathematics at the Institute for Advanced Study here, Dr. Einstein was born at Ulm, Germany, on March 14, 1879. He was a Nobel Prize win-

---

18th April– Albert Einstein passed away at Princeton Hospital, NJ. The German-born theoretical physicist had been admitted one day earlier with internal bleeding accompanied by severe pain, caused by a burst abdominal aortic aneurysm. He was 76-years-old.

Regarded as one of the most brilliant minds of the modern era, Einstein was most famous for developing the theory of relativity, and for the mass-energy formula $E=mc^2$.

In 1921 he was awarded the Nobel Prize in Physics for his discovery of the law of the photoelectric effect.

Helen Dukas, Einstein's long-time secretary and companion, recounted him saying: "You're really hysterical—I have to pass on sometime, and it doesn't really matter when." He died peacefully the next morning.

Coup d'état Ousts Perón

16th September– Argentinian President Juan Domingo Perón was ousted following a violent coup, resulting in a military dictatorship for Argentina, and exile for Perón. He would return to Argentina in 1973, winning the presidency again later that year.

Populist Perón began his first presidency in 1946, winning with promises of social justice and economic independence.

He is remembered for his record investments in health care, public works and housing construction. And for his efforts to stimulate industrial growth, increase workers' pay, and reduce poverty and unemployment. His political ideals were neither capitalist nor socialist, but a unique blend of nationalism and populism known as Perónism, a movement which continues to this day.

Although being extremely popular, Perón was intolerant of opposition, resorting to violence and fascist rule to maintain control. He was opposed by the middle classes, intelligentsia, and the church.

In 1955, controversial new reforms to legalize divorce and prostitution spurred his opposers to take action. Following a bomb attack killing 364 supporters, Perónists retaliated by burning several churches.

Perón is also remembered for his beautiful second wife, Eva, who was adored by the people for her political activities on behalf of women, the poor and the working-class.

Cinema and Films of 1955

Kim Novak & James Stewart in *Vertigo* (Paramount Pictures, 1958).

With television becoming ever more commonplace in American homes, cinema attendance faced a steady decline throughout the 1950s. In order to win over new audiences, the motion picture industry sought the attention of younger viewers who had more leisure time and cash to spare.

The early to mid 50s brought a new wave of exciting, young, sexy, anti-hero stars, such as Marlon Brando, James Dean, Kim Novak, Marilyn Monroe and Paul Newman.

Highest Paid Stars

1   James Stewart
2   Grace Kelly
3   John Wayne
4   William Holden
5   Gary Cooper
6   Marilyn Monroe
7   Dean Martin &
    Jerry Lewis
8   Marlon Brando
9   Humphrey Bogart
10 Clark Gable

Clint Eastwood in 1955.

Paul Newman in 1954.

1955 film debuts

Clint Eastwood	Revenge of the Creature
Shirley MacLaine	The Trouble with Harry
Jayne Mansfield	Female Jungle
Walter Matthau	The Kentuckian
Shirley Jones	Oklahoma!
Joanne Woodward	Count Three and Pray

* From en.wikipedia.org/wiki/1955_in_film.

Top Grossing Films of 1955

1	Cinerama Holiday	Cinerama Production	$10,000,000
2	Mister Roberts	Warner Bros.	$8,500,000
3	Battle Cry	Warner Bros.	$8,100,000
4	Oklahoma!	RKO	$7,100,000
5	Guys and Dolls	MGM	$6,801,000
6	Lady and the Tramp	Disney	$6,500,000
7	Picnic	Columbia	$6,300,000
8	Not as a Stranger	United Artists	$6,200,000
9	Strategic Air Command	Paramount	$6,000,000
=	The Seven Year Itch	20th Century Fox	$6,000,000
=	The Sea Chase	Warner Bros.	$6,000,000
=	To Hell and Back	Universal Pictures	$6,000,000
10	I'll Cry Tomorrow	MGM	$5,873,000

* From en.wikipedia.org/wiki/1955_in_film
by box office gross in the USA.

Marilyn Monroe's 23rd film, *The Seven Year Itch*, is most notably remembered for her white dress billowing over a New York subway grate scene.

Disney's 15th animated feature film, *Lady and the Tramp*, was their first to be filmed in new widescreen Cinemascope.

FIBERGLAS GLAMOUR MARQUISETTES

White as angels. Finer than sugarspun. *Guaranteed no-ironing because they're Coronized!**

Your windows can have this heavenly white look . . . and *keep* it. Not only do the new Fiberglas marquisettes look as fabulous as debutante ball gowns . . . they also *shed dirt* the way crystal sheds dirt. Coronizing, a new miracle process, makes them work-proof. They wash to a bright white . . . and hang dry in 7 minutes . . . without a touch of ironing, even at ruffles and hems. They're shrink-proof, stretch-proof, mildew-proof, fire-proof. And let the sun blaze! Fiberglas marquisettes stay fresh and crisp in a sizzling sunshine. Now in all sizes and styles. Owens-Corning Fiberglas, Decorative Fabrics, 598 Madison Avenue, New York 22, N. Y.

makes good things better
...makes new things possible

White as angels. Finer than sugarspun. *Guaranteed no-ironing because they're Coronized!*

Your windows can have this heavenly white look... and *keep* it. Not only do the new Fiberglas marquisettes look as fabulous as debutante ball gowns... they also *shed dirt* the way crystal sheds dirt. Coronizing, a new miracle process, makes them work-proof. They wash to a bright white... and hang dry in 7 minutes... without a touch of ironing, even at ruffles and hems. They're shrink-proof, stretch-proof, mildew-proof, fire-proof. And let the sun blaze! Fiberglas marquisettes stay fresh and crisp in a sizzling sunshine. Now in all sizes and styles. Owens-Corning Fiberglas, Decorative Fabrics, 598 Madison Avenue, New York 22, N.Y.

Cat on a Hot Tin Roof Opens on Broadway

Broadway classic *Cat on a Hot Tin Roof*, based on the Pulitzer Prize-winning book by Tennessee Williams, premiered on 24th March 1955 at the Morosco Theater in New York City. The same year it would receive four Tony nominations and win the Best Drama awards at the Pulitzer Prize and the New York Drama Critics' Circle.

The three-act play opened in London in 1958 and has since seen several Broadway and international revivals.

Theatrical poster from 1955.

Cinema poster from 1958 (MGM).

Barbara Bel Geddes and Ben Gazzara in the original Broadway cast, *Cat on a Hot Tin Roof*, 1955. Elizabeth Taylor and Paul Newman in the 1958 film.

The 1958 movie version would star Elizabeth Taylor and Paul Newman, two of Hollywood's biggest names, in the leading roles. Most of the book's homosexual themes were removed for the film, which greatly angered Williams.

James Dean–Death of an Icon

Actor James Dean was killed in a head-on collision in Cholame, California, at 4:45pm on 30th September 1955.

His death was announced the next day in newspapers, radio and TV, sending shock waves across the country and catapulting the rising young star to cult status. He remains forever frozen as a symbol of teenage angst. He was only 24 years old.

Remains of Dean's Porche 550 Spyder after the crash.

James Dean in his brand new Porche.

Dean was driving his new Porsche 550 Spyder convertible to Salinas, California, to indulge in his passion for car racing.

Unable to race during filming, Dean was quick to enter the 1st October Salinas Road Race event as soon as filming on his third movie was completed. The collision occurred at an intersection with a left-turning truck. The truck driver and Dean's driving companion both survived the crash. Dean died instantly from a broken neck.

During Dean's short but brilliant acting career he starred in only three major Hollywood films.

In his first film, *East of Eden* (Warner Bros. 1955), Dean portrayed the role of a troubled young teen. Improvising many of the unscripted, deeply emotional scenes, he would be posthumously nominated for an Academy Award the following year.

Dean's second film, *Rebel Without a Cause* (Warner Bros. 1955), would secure his iconic status in American youth culture. As high-school misfit Jim Stark, Dean gave young viewers a hero they could relate to.

Dean starred alongside Rock Hudson and Elizabeth Taylor in his third film, *Giant* (Warner Bros. 1956). Released after his death, the film would earn Dean his second posthumous Academy Award nomination.

At last—the thrill of fine stereo
at a moderate price
New Kodak Stereo Camera only $84⁵⁰

Kodak's new stereo camera is quality through and through, yet costs about half of what you'd expect to have to pay.

What's more, you'll find yourself making excellent 3-dimensional shots with your very first roll. Kodak designers have simplified controls to an astonishing degree. Actually, stereo pictures with the Kodak Stereo Camera are as easy to take as ordinary snapshots. Brilliant f/3.5 lenses, shutter speeds to 1/200, many automatic features—all for a modest $84.50, including Federal Tax.

And 2 superb new viewers with handy focusing controls and adjustable eyepieces. Kodaslide Stereo Viewer I, battery-operated, $12.75. Kodaslide Stereo Viewer II plugs into house circuit, has exclusive brightness control—$23.75. Most Kodak dealers offer convenient terms.

Prices subject to change without notice

Eastman Kodak Company, Rochester 4, N. Y.

Kodak

Kodak's new stereo camera is quality through and through, yet costs about half of what you'd expect to have to pay.

What's more, you'll find yourself making excellent 3-dimensional shots with your very first roll. Kodak designers have simplified controls to an astonishing degree. Actually, stereo pictures with the Kodak Stereo Camera are as easy to take as ordinary snapshots. Brilliant f/3.5 lenses, shutter speeds to 1/200, many automatic features—all for a modest $84.50, including Federal Tax.

And 2 superb new viewers with handy focusing controls and adjustable eyepieces. Kodaslide Stereo Viewer I, battery-operated, $12.75. Kodaslide Stereo Viewer II plugs into house circuit, has exclusive brightness control—$23.75. Most Kodak dealers offer convenient terms.

Thousands say this is the simplest, surest personal movie camera ever made. With it, folks everywhere are already enjoying family movies.

The Brownie has just one simple setting to make—then aim, press the button and you're making movies! Capturing your family good times in all their *action*... all their *color*... as only movies can.

And don't let the low price of the Brownie fool you, either. New simplified design, plus the Brownie's great popularity, helps us keep costs down. The Brownie is *all* camera, handsomely and ruggedly constructed for years of happy service.

Ask your dealer to show you the Brownie Movie Camera soon. (Or send coupon for free booklet.) And ask him about convenient terms, too. Most Kodak dealers offer them.

Disneyland's Grand Opening

17th July 1955

Visitors at Sleeping Beauty's castle.

Original Mickey and Donald costumes, 17th July 1955.

Walt Disney at the opening ceremony. "To all who come to this happy place— welcome. Disneyland is your land."

Disneyland, Walt Disney's "folly" of fun, fantasy and futurism, opened its doors on 17th July 1955 for a special press preview. Chaos ensued after thousands of counterfeit tickets were sold. Uncontrollable crowds stormed the attractions, food and drink ran out, and underprepared facilities struggled to accommodate the hoards of excited attendees.

After several years of planning, the ambitious $17 million project was constructed in just one year on 16 acres in Anaheim, California. Despite its disastrous opening day, workers ensured all the park attractions were running smoothly within the month. And by the second month of operation, it was reported that 1 million people had visited. For most, it was and still is, "the happiest place on earth."

An estimated 70 million people tuned in to watch ABC TVs 90-minute live broadcast of the star-studded opening ceremonies, co-hosted by Ronald Regan.

YOU'LL CALL IT "MILK MAGIC" -NEW INSTANT STARLAC

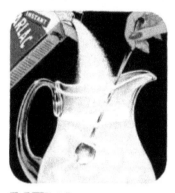

NEW Mixes instantly even in ice water!

NEW It tastes so good, you'll hardly believe you made it from a powder!

NEW true milk-sweet taste when compared with other brands

"**The most exciting thing** that's ever happened to milk," you'll say when you first try New Instant Starlac.

Think of it! You get all the proteins, B vitamins and calcium of the finest pasteurized milk for only about 8¢ a quart. What a saving! What a wonderful way to bring life-giving nourishment to your family at a low, low price!

This wonderful New Instant Starlac is put out by The Borden Company, the most famous name in milk, a company which has pioneered milk improvements for more than 100 years. Try New Instant Starlac. Get it at your grocer's today.

Use Borden's new-type nonfat milk for drinking, cooking and baking.

In big blue economy 5-qt. pkg. for...

NEW packages... blue 5qt. economy size... red 3qt pre-measured.

NEW all new...mixes instantly, tastes better... you'll call it "Milk Magic"

about 8¢ a quart

In red 3-qt. pre-measured envelope pkg. at a slightly higher price.

"The most exciting thing that's ever happened to milk," you'll say when you first try New Instant Starlac.

Think of it! You get all the proteins, B vitamins and calcium of the finest pasteurized milk for only about 8¢ a quart. What a saving! What a wonderful way to bring life-giving nourishment to your family at a low, low price!

This wonderful New Instant Starlac is put out by The Borden Company, the most famous name in milk, a company which has pioneered milk improvements for more than 100 years. Try New instant Starlac. Get it at your grocer's today.

Use Borden's new-type nonfat milk for drinking, cooking and baking.

In big blue economy 5-qt. pkg. for... about 8¢ a quart.
In red 3-qt. pre-measured envelope pkg. at a slightly higher price.

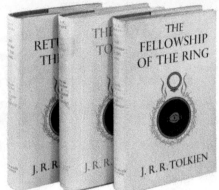

The Lord of the Rings, a series of three fantasy novels written by English author J.R.R. Tolkien, was conceived as a sequel to his 1937 novel *The Hobbit*.

Originally written as one volume, the work was published as a trilogy in 1954-55 in the UK, and 1955-56 in the USA.

The Lord of the Rings immediate success was credited with the growing popularity of the fantasy genre from the 50s and 60s till the present day. Its influence on popular culture has been wide ranging, spawning many imitators in film, literature and video-gaming.

From 2001-2003 the books were released as a film series directed by Peter Jackson. Shot entirely in New Zealand, the films were a major critical and financial success. Each film garnered several Academy Awards, placing them amongst the greatest film trilogies ever made.

The Lord of the Rings has been translated in 38 different languages and sold over 150 million copies, remaining popular till this day. The books have been adapted for radio, theater, television and film. In 2003, the trilogy was awarded BBC's Best British novel of all time.

The first *Guinness Book of Records* arrived in bookstores across the UK on 27th August 1955. By Christmas it had become a crowd favorite and hot best seller. The second edition, released one year later, sold an astonishing 70,000 copies in the USA alone.

Sir Hugh Beaver, then the managing director of the Guinness Breweries, conceived the idea of a reference book to help settle nightly pub debates. The book would be filled with world records of human (and non-human) achievements.

Due to its immediate success, further books were released in the following years, settling into a pattern of one book per year.

Now known as *Guinness World Records*, the book itself holds the record of the best-selling copyrighted book of all time. It is published in 23 languages in over 100 countries, spawning multiple TV shows and franchised museums worldwide.

FOREWORD

By the Rt. Hon. the Earl of Iveagh K.G., C.B., C.M.G.

•

Wherever people congregate to talk, they will argue, and sometimes the joy lies in the arguing and would be lost if there were any definite answer. But more often the argument takes place on a dispute of fact, and it can be very exasperating if there is no immediate means of settling the argument. Who was the first to swim the Channel? Where is England's deepest well, or Scotland's highest tree, or Ireland's oldest church? How many died in history's worst rail crash? Who gained the biggest majority in Parliament? What is the highest point in our county? What is the greatest weight a man has ever lifted? And so on. How much heat these innocent questions can raise! Guinness in producing this book hopes that it may assist in resolving many such disputes, and may, we hope, turn heat into light.

Iveagh

Chairman

Arthur Guinness Son & Co., Ltd.,
Park Royal Brewery,
London

August 1955

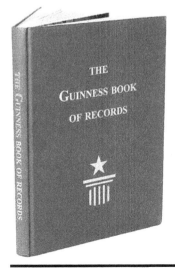

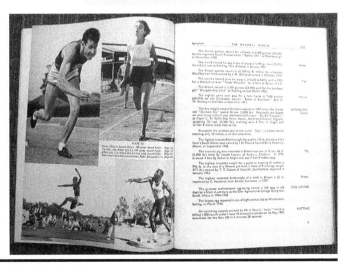

Going away on a trip?

Make your plans by Long Distance

You're off to a more pleasant trip when you telephone ahead.

A Long Distance call is the quickest, friendliest way to let folks know how you're coming . . . and when you'll arrive.

While you're away, a regular voice-visit across the miles will help you keep in close touch with home. It means so much. Costs so little.

Someone, somewhere, would like to hear your voice right now.

LONG DISTANCE RATES ARE LOW

Here are some examples:

New York to Philadelphia . . 40¢
Pittsburgh to Cleveland . . 45¢
St. Louis to Cincinnati . . . 75¢
Atlanta to Chicago $1.05
Seattle to Washington, D. C. . $2.00

These are the Station-to-Station rates for the first three minutes, after 6 o'clock every night and all day Sunday. They do not include the 10% federal excise tax.

CALL BY NUMBER. IT'S TWICE AS FAST.

BELL TELEPHONE SYSTEM

A Rock 'n' Roll Revolution

Rock 'n' Roll exploded onto our soundwaves in the mid-fifties, and took the world by storm. The energy, the rhythm, the emotion—we had never heard anything quite like it before. Parents were alarmed and appalled in equal measure. It sprang from the ghettos of small town shop-front record studios while the big city record labels were napping.

Rock 'n' Roll was the first music ever created specifically for teenagers. The first of the Baby Boomers had found their sound. It was neither black nor white. It gave expression to youth of any race and social status. It was a mash of rhythm & blues, country & western, gospel, hill-billy, blues, and jazz, with a heavy rock beat.

Chuck Berry, Fats Domino, Bill Haley and his Comets, Jerry Lee Lewis, and of course Elvis, became household names.

Jerry Lee Lewis.

Bill Haley and His Comets.

25th March 1955– *Blackboard Jungle* debuted with Bill Haley and his Comets *Rock Around the Clock* playing during the opening credits. The movie's soundtrack saw the largely teenage audience dancing in the aisles during screenings. This date is widely recognised as marking the birth of rock 'n' roll.

Sun Records in Memphis TN. was home to many rock 'n' roll greats, including Elvis Presley, Jerry Lee Lewis, Carl Perkins, Jonny Cash, Roy Orbison, Howlin' Wolf, and The Dixie Cups.

Billboard Top 30 Songs of 1955

	Artist	Song Title
1	Perez Prado	Cherry Pink And Apple Blossom White
2	Bill Haley & His Comets	Rock Around the Clock
3	Mitch Miller	The Yellow Rose of Texas
4	Roger Williams	Autumn Leaves
5	Les Baxter	Unchained Melody
6	Bill Hayes	The Ballad of Davy Crockett
7	The Four Aces	Love Is a Many-Splendored Thing
8	The McGuire Sisters	Sincerely
9	Pat Boone	Ain't That a Shame
10	Georgia Gibbs	The Wallflower (Dance with Me, Henry)

Perez Prado.

Bill Haley and His Comets.

Pat Boone.

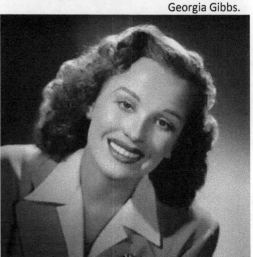

Georgia Gibbs.

	Artist	Song Title
11	Johnny Maddox	The Crazy Otto Medley
12	Billy Vaughn	Melody of Love
13	Tennessee Ernie Ford	Sixteen Tons
14	Frank Sinatra	Learnin' the Blues
15	The Fontane Sisters	Hearts of Stone
16	Georgia Gibbs	Tweedle Dee
17	The Four Lads	Moments to Remember
18	The Chordettes	Mr. Sandman
19	Joan Weber	Let Me Go, Lover!
20	Nat King Cole	A Blossom Fell

Frank Sinatra.

Nat King Cole.

21	Al Hibbler	Unchained Melody
22	Fess Parker	The Ballad of Davy Crockett
23	Art Mooney	Honey-Babe
24	Tennessee Ernie Ford	The Ballad of Davy Crockett
25	Perry Como	Ko Ko Mo (I Love You So)
26	Gisele MacKenzie	Hard to Get
27	Ames Brothers	The Naughty Lady of Shady Lane
28	Jaye P. Morgan	That's All I Want from You
29	The Platters	Only You (And You Alone)
30	Somethin' Smith and the Redheads	It's a Sin to Tell a Lie

* From the *Billboard* top 30 singles of 1955.

fashion's New pet ... our

Poodle Print
only 5.98

Fashion's pet . . . and yours! Our adorable new border "poodle print", is the cutest thing around town! "Stop-look" styling . . . with curved lines, tiny middle and big tiered skirt.

You'll love it for movie dates . . . informal parties. It's sure to rate with the crowd . . . send admiring glances your way. Big fashion . . . the little price? Only $5.98!

GUARANTEED
WASHABLE

Style 621
ONE-PIECE

Fabric: Poodle Print Cotton
Color: Navy with Contrasting Print
Junior Sizes: 9, 11, 13, 15, 17
Lengths: 44½, 44½, 45, 45, 45½

Price $5.98
Deposit . . . 1.00
Balance . . . 4.98
(Plus postage and C. O. D. fees)

ECONOMY FEATURE
Any 2—$5.98 Dresses for only $11.49; Deposit $2.90
(Plus postage and C. O. D. fees)

Fashion Frocks Inc.
CINCINNATI, OHIO

Navy

Fabric: Poodle Print Cotton

Fashion's pet... and yours! Our adorable new border "poodle print" is the cutest thing around town! "Stop-look" styling...with curved lines, tiny middle and big tiered skirt.

You'll have it for movie dates...informal parties. It's sure to rate with the crowd...send admiring glances your way. Big fashion...the little price? Only $5.98!

Fashion Trends of the 1950s

With the penny-pinching misery and bleakness of the war years long forgotten, the 1950s were a time to show off. And nowhere was this more apparent than through our fashion choices. The pinched waist look of the late 40s carried throughout the 50s decade. Our clothes allowed us to express beauty, excellence, luxury and extravagance.

Fashion of the 50s was highlighted by a clear gender divide. While women's fashion focused on femininity and tailored formality, men's fashion embraced the casual and cool of working class daywear.

a
FERNFIELD
fashion

By 1955, dresses and skirts reached voluminous proportions with pleats and folds flaunting an abundance of fabric.

Christian Dior's "New Look" from 1947.

Day wear and evening wear for women on both sides of the Atlantic continued to take its direction from the haute couture salons of Paris. Christian Dior's "New Look", unveiled in 1947, set the standard for the entire decade of the 1950s.

Gone were the boxy tailored jackets with padded shoulders and short skirts. Dior had brought back femininity, with clinched waists, fuller busts and hips, and longer, wider skirts. The emphasis was on abundance.

Christian Dior's "New Look" from 1955.

To achieve this impossible hour-glass figure, corsets and girdles were sold in record numbers. Metal underwire bras made a comeback, and a new form of bra known as the "cathedral bra" or "bullet bra" became popular.

The Bullet Bra from Exquisite Form in 1955.

Women embraced the femininity of 1950s' fashion from head to toe. Hats, scarves, belts, gloves, shoes, stockings, handbags and jewelry were all given due consideration.

Out on the street, no outfit was complete without a full complement of matching accessories.

It's simply <u>wicked</u> what it does for you

Care to be daring, darling? To look outright naughty, yet feel downright nice? Then why not give in to that inner whisper, and agree to star in this exciting new vehicle.

You'll get all the best lines... all the admiring looks—in your most demanding clothes. Your entrances? Positively breathtaking. Because Warner's knows every beautiful scene-stealing way to keep you in the center of the stage.

Once you taste the spotlights and applause, you'll never go anywhere *important* without your Merry Widow. Here just two of the famous supporting cast. Try the feeling today! From $3.50 at the nicest stores here and in Canada.

#1311. (*Right*) The fabulous original... for a hand-span waist, a grand-stand look. Cuffs turn down or up. Black or white embroidered nylon and elastic marquisette, $12.50.

#1317. (*Left*) The waist a little easier, the lines a little longer; the bust high, round, and youthful for the newest dresses. Black or white embroidered nylon marquisette. $15.00.

Despite criticisms against the extravagance of the New Look, and arguments that heavy corsets and paddings undermined the freedoms women had won during the war years, the New Look was embraced on both sides of the Atlantic.

FIRST IN FASHION ... the Romantic Color

The color is Turquoise ... clear, cool, delicious looking in a beautiful collection to take you whirling through spring and summer

Dresses from the Spiegel Spring-Summer Home Shopping Book, 1955.

Clothing manufacturers produced stylish, ready-to-wear clothes for the masses. Inexpensive versions of Dior's New Look in florals and pretty pastels filled our closets and graced our suburban homes and streets. No longer just for the wealthy, the growing middle classes could now afford to be fashionable. Magazines and mail-order catalogs were sure to keep us informed of the latest in fashion and accessories.

You can get a smoother tan...faster with Skol's exclusive formula

Tan gloriously

your first day in the sun
...with **SKOL'S** sun-control screen

- you don't burn
- you don't peel
- no messy oil

Skol's sun-control screen actually *regulates* the sun's effect on your skin. It shuts out the harmful burning rays. Lets in the beneficial tanning rays. Speeds up the whole tanning process—*more safely*.

You tan comfortably

Not a trace of oil or grease to get on your suit or towel or beach bag. Skol goes on cleanly, neatly. Doesn't pick up sand. And Skol is kind to your skin. Skol won't dry out natural moisture. Won't leave your skin feeling drawn and "tight."

More people tan with Skol

Originally formulated for Alpine guides to prevent dreaded "snow-burn," Skol has become the leading sun product throughout the world. Swimmers, golfers, skiers, all people who play and work in the sun choose Skol above all others.

Use the new Skol this summer. You'll tan *faster* ... in a day or a weekend. More *beautifully* ... and safely. Get your bottle of Skol today. Also available in plastic bottles.

Skol's sun-control screen actually *regulates* the sun's effect on your skin. It shuts out the harmful burning rays. Lets in the beneficial tanning rays. Speeds up the whole tanning process—more *safely*.

You tan comfortable.

Not a trace of oil or grease to get on your suit or towel or beach bag. Skol goes on cleanly, neatly. Doesn't pick up sand. And Skol is kind to your skin. Skol won't dry out natural moisture. Won't leave your skin feeling drawn and "tight."

More people tan with Skol.

Originally formulated for Alpine guides to prevent dreaded "snow-burn," Skol has become the leading sun product throughout the world. Swimmers, golfers, skiers, all people who play and work in the sun choose Skol above all others.

Use the new Skol this summer. You'll tan *faster*... in a day or a weekend. More *beautifully*... and safely. Get your bottle of Skol today. Also available in plastic bottles.

Dior also created a slimmed down alternative look, widely copied by other designers in ready-to-wear and pattern books. This figure-hugging groomed and tailored look continued to place emphasis on the hourglass figure, and was suitable for day or evening dress, or as an elegant straight skirt and short jacket.

Known as the "sheath dress" or "wiggle dress", this sexier silhouette was preferred by movie stars such as Jane Russell and Marilyn Monroe.

Model wears Dior inspired outfit by Forstmann.
Dress patterns by Advance.

Marilyn Monroe in 1955.

Not much changed in the world of men's fashion during the 1950s. Business attire shifted just a little. Suits were slimmer, and ties were narrower. Skinny belts were worn over pleated pants. Hats, though still worn, were on the way out.

Marlon Brando.

Frank Sinatra.

James Dean.

For the younger generation however, the fashion icons of the day set the trends. James Dean and Marlon Brando made the white T-shirt and blue jeans the must-have items in casual attire. Worn alone, or under an unbuttoned shirt or jacket, the look made working class style a middle-class fashion statement.

Surprise! It's liltingly light, yet lusciously bright!

We fervently feel that pink is for girls...and a million men agree with us! "Love That Pink!"...not a shy pink...a showoff pink! Not a whisper pink, a whistle pink! It's light, yet it's bright (what a beautiful paradox!) No matter what your coloring, this is your color! Whether you're petal-pale or brown as bronze, wear "Love That Pink" tonight...you'll hear the excitement crackling, clear across the room!

"Love That Pink" Lanolite Lipstick 1.10* (Only non-smear type lipstick especially made to soften your lips and keep them moist) "Love That Pink" Nail Enamel .60*

*PLUS TAX

© 1955 REVLON PRODUCTS CORP.

Surprise! It's liltingly <u>light</u>, yet lusciously <u>bright</u>!

We fervently feel that pink is for girls...and a million men agree with us! "Love That Pink!" ...not a shy pink...a <u>showoff</u> pink! Not a whisper pink, a <u>whistle</u> pink! It's light, yet it's bright (what a beautiful paradox!) No matter what your coloring, this is your color! Whether you're petal-pale or brown as bronze, wear "Love That Pink" tonight...you'll <u>hear</u> the excitement crackling, clear across the room!

A Vaccine for Polio

During the first half of the 20th Century the dreaded poliomyelitis virus (polio) caused frequent epidemics throughout the industrialized world. The virus appeared during the summer months, attacking mostly the young, causing muscle weakness, paralysis and death.

Jonas Salk's polio vaccine, widely tested in field trials during the preceding year, was declared safe for use on 12th April 1955. A nationwide inoculation program began in the USA, reducing the number of polio cases by 90% within just two years.

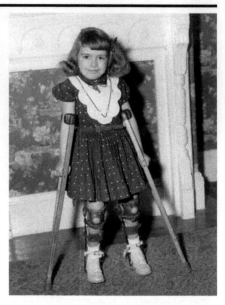

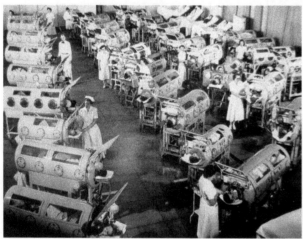

Rows of polio patients in their iron lungs at the Rancho Los Amigos hospital in Downey, Calif. 1953.

At its peak in the 40s and 50s, polio affected many thousands of people each year. Use of the "iron lung" a pressure chamber to aid breathing, saved the lives of those with infected lungs. Patients were encased within for months, years, or even for life.

To save on floor space within polio wards, children were placed in iron lung "pods"– multi-person negative-pressure ventilators.

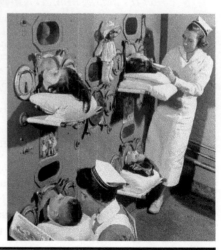

Worldwide polio eradication is still an ongoing struggle, as some developing countries continue to see yearly outbreaks of the virus. Civil wars, ignorance, and government distrust prevent large scale vaccination programs from succeeding.

Science and Medicine

15th Feb– Howard Tracy Hall, working for the General Electric Company, announced the successful creation of synthetic diamonds in the scientific journal *Nature*, with a reproducible, verifiable and well-documented process.

15th Mar– The United States Air Force unveiled its first supersonic air-to-surface self-guided missile–the GAM-63 RASCAL.

The RASCAL required an air-launch above 40,000 feet (12,000 m). A computer within tracked the aircraft position against a pre-programmed target, automatically releasing the missile at the launch point. The missile would continue climbing for a certain distance, before diving on its target.

7th Aug– Sony began selling the TR-55 transistor radio–the first commercial transistor radio to utilize all miniature components.

11th Oct– *Oklahoma!* debuted using the new 70-mm wide film system known as the Todd-AO. Developed by producer Mike Todd, the 70mm was much cheaper to run than its wide film predecessor Cinerama.

1955– The first cesium based atomic clock was built at the National Physical Laboratory, UK. by Louis Essen and Jack Parry. The clock became commercially available, for use as a calibration source, the following year. It cost $20,000.

Other news from 1955

Now...Coke *in* Family-Size, *too!*

1955– Coca-Cola expanded its size offerings introducing bottles in 10-, 12-, 16-, and 26-ounce sizes. Before this, only the standard 6.5-ounce bottle had been available. Coke also began manufacturing its first canned drinks for sale to overseas armed services. A protective polymer lining added to the inside of the can prevented the steel from acid erosion.

2nd Jan– Panamanian president José Antonio Remón was assassinated by three assailants armed with sub-machine guns. His successor, José Ramón Guizado, was later arrested for orchestrating the assassination. Guizado would spend thirty-three months in jail before being acquitted.

17th Jan– USS Nautilus (SSN-571) became the world's first nuclear powered submarine. Able to remain submerged longer than traditional diesel-electric submarines, she could travel to depths previously unattainable, and cruise at faster speed.

24th Feb– Severe weather in Britain plunged temperatures below freezing leaving more than 70 roads blocked with snow and Country rail services canceled. Snowdrifts as high as 30ft (9m) were recorded.

1st Mar– Pakistan and India drew in the 5th cricket Test at the National Stadium in Karachi; 5 Test series, score 0-0.

5th Apr– British Prime Minister Winston Churchill resigned due to ill-health at the age of 80. Churchill had served as Prime Minister from 1940-1945, and again from 1951-1955.

11th Apr– An assassination attempt on Premier Zhou Enlai left sixteen dead when a bomb exploded on the chartered plane supposed to be carrying the Chinese leader. He was not on board.

6th Jun– British Parliament introduced the Harmful Publications Act, aimed at protecting children from violent, repulsive or horror comics.

5th May– 10 years after the end of WWII, West Germany was granted full sovereignty by its three occupying Allied powers. Military occupation ended, and West Germany joined NATO on 9th May 1955.

11th Jun– Eighty-three spectators were killed and 180 more injured after two race cars collided in the 24 Hours of Le Mans, France. Flying and burning debris were hurled into the stands at high speed. The race remains known as auto-racing's deadliest day.

15th Sep– Vladimir Nabokov's controversial novel Lolita was published by Olympia Press, Paris. The book was soon banned in France and the UK. It sold 100,000 copies in its first three weeks of release in the USA in 1958.

The novel has since been adapted for stage, film, ballet, opera and Broadway.

22nd Sep– Commercial television started in the UK when the Independent Television Authority's (ITV) began broadcasting in London, ending the BBC monopoly.

How to avoid dry, unruly "jungle hair"

New <u>greaseless</u> way to keep your hair neat all day

New Vitalis with V-7 prevents dryness, makes hair easy to manage

If you dislike over-oily hair tonics, here's good news. New Vitalis keeps hair in place with V-7, the *greaseless* grooming discovery.

You can use Vitalis as often as you like—even every day—yet never have an over-slick, plastered-down look.

What's more, it gives you wonderful protection from dry hair and scalp. And tests show it kills on contact germs many doctors associate with infectious dandruff—as no mere cream or oil dressing can.

Try new Vitalis with V-7. You'll *like* it.

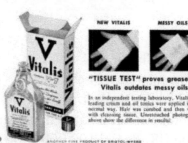

NEW VITALIS   **MESSY OILS**

"TISSUE TEST" **proves greaseless Vitalis outdates messy oils**

In an independent testing laboratory, Vitalis and leading cream and oil tonics were applied in the normal way. Hair was combed and then wiped with cleansing tissue. Unretouched photographs above show the difference in results!

New VITALIS® Hair Tonic with V-7®

ANOTHER FINE PRODUCT OF BRISTOL-MYERS

New Vitalis with V-7 prevents dryness, makes hair easy to mange.

If you dislike over-oily hair tonics, here's good news. New Vitalis keeps hair in place with V-7, the *greaseless* grooming discovery.

You can use Vitalis as often as you like–even every day–yet never have an over-slick, plastered-down look.

What's more, it gives you wonderful protection from dry hair and scalp. And tests show it kills on contact germs many doctors associate with infectious dandruff–as no mere cream or oil dressing can.

Try new Vitalis with V-7. You'll *like* it.

"Tissue Test" proves greaseless Vitalis outdates messy oils.

In an independent testing laboratory, Vitalis and leading cream and oil tonics were applied in the normal way. Hair was combed and then wiped with cleansing tissue. Unretouched photographs above show the difference in results!

"Is this something special?"
"It certainly is... that's Ballantine Ale"

The sociable beverage that's more and more in evidence at friendly gatherings is Ballantine...
the *different* ale.

In Ballantine, the time-honored flavor of ale... and the lightness and liveliness Americans
prefer in their brewed beverages... are so happily married that it has won a very special place in
the affections of millions.

The sooner you try it, the longer you'll have to enjoy it. Get acquainted with this great ale
today; it gives you so much more in flavor... and satisfaction... *it's America's favorite by four to
one.*

Famous people born in 1955

6th Jan– Rowan Atkinson, English comedian & actor.

18th Jan– Kevin Costner, American actor, producer & director.

28th Jan– Nicolas Sarkozy, 23rd President of France.

8th Feb– John Grisham, American writer, attorney & politician.

10th Feb– Greg Norman, Australian golfer.

21st Feb– Kelsey Grammer, American actor & comedian.

24th Feb– Alain Prost, French Formula One racing driver.

24th Feb– Steve Jobs, American computer entrepreneur & co-founder of Apple.

5th Mar– Penn Jillette, American author and magician (Penn & Teller).

19th Mar– Bruce Willis, American actor.

23rd Mar– Moses Malone, Basketball Hall of Fame center .

31st Mar– Angus Young, Scottish Australian, rock guitarist (ACDC).

15th Apr– Dodi Fayed, Egyptian businessman.

23rd Apr– Judy Davis, Australian actress.

2nd May– Donatella Versace, Italian fashion designer.

3rd May– David Hookes, Australian cricketer.

16th May– Jack Morris, Baseball Hall of Fame pitcher.

18th May– Chow Yun-Fat, Hong Kong actor.

7th Jun– William Forsythe, American actor.

8th Jun– Tim Berners-Lee, English inventor of the World Wide Web.

22nd Jul– Willem Dafoe, American actor.

25th Jul– Iman Abdulmajid, Somalian fashion model.

4th Aug– Billy Bob Thornton, American actor, director & screenwriter.

13th Aug– Betsy King, American golfer.

15th Sep– Renzo Rosso, Italian clothing designer.

28th Oct– Bill Gates, American businessman.

6th Nov– Maria Shriver, American newscaster.

13th Nov– Whoopi Goldberg, American actress & comedian.

24th Nov– Ian Botham, England cricket captain, all-rounder.

27th Nov– Bill Nye, the Science Guy, TV Host.

29th Nov– Howie Mandel, comedian.

30th Nov– Billy Idol, [William Broad], rocker.

A new fine-strand spaghetti with beefy little <u>meatballs</u>—by Franco-American

MY GOODNESS, hadn't you heard? Here's a brand-new FRANCO-AMERICAN dish that's different from anything you've ever tasted. Different, and (forgive us for bragging) terrific! It's our special new Spaghetti with Meatballs.

This is a *fine-strand* spaghetti—the kind you like so much—in a tantalizing new tomato sauce.

But the best news is about those tender, beefy little meatballs you see in our picture. They're *already in the Spaghetti*. *Four* of them—count 'em, four—in every single can!

This is a *meal*, Mothers. Mighty nutritious eating, too. Don't forget that every helping supplies *proteins* and *energy* which growing children and grownups need every day.

Like all your old Franco-American favorites, this newest treat is a cinch to fix. You simply heat it for about 3 minutes, serve, and get ready to say, "Thank you," for all the compliments you'll get.

Economical? Very agreeably so. It costs less than 15¢ a serving.

Spaghetti with Meatballs
BY FRANCO-AMERICAN

My goodness, hadn't you heard? Here's a brand-new Franco-American dish that's different from anything you've ever tasted. Different, and (forgive us for bragging) terrific! It's our special new Spaghetti with Meatballs.

This is a *fine-strand* spaghetti–the kind you like so much–in a tantalizing new tomato sauce.

But the best news is about those tender, beefy little meatballs you see in our picture. They're *already in the Spaghetti*. *Four* of them–count 'em, four–in every single can!

This is a *meal*, Mothers. Mighty nutritious eating, too. Don't forget that every helping supplies *proteins* and *energy* which growing children and grownups need every day.

Like all your old Franco-American favorites, this newest treat is a cinch to fix. You simply heat it for about 3 minutes, serve, and get ready to say, "Thank you," for all the compliments you'll get.

Economical? Very agreeably so. It costs less than 15¢ a serving.

1955 in Numbers

Statistics [1]

• Population of the world	2.77 billion
• Population in the United States	171.69 million
• Population in the United Kingdom	51.06 million
• Population in Canada	15.67 million
• Population in Australia	9.17 million
• Average age for marriage of women	20.2 years old
• Average age for marriage of men	22.6 years old
• USA divorce rate	23%
• Average family income USA	$4,400 per year
• Minimum wage USA	$0.75 per hour

Costs of Goods [2]

• Average home	$10,950
• Average new car	$1,900
• Studebaker Commander Coupe	$2,095
• A gallon of gas	$0.23
• A loaf of bread	$0.18
• A gallon of milk	$0.92
• Oreo cookies	$0.39 per pkg
• Sirloin chops	$0.69 per pound
• Starkist tuna	$0.25 per 6.5 oz can
• Potatoes	$0.53 for 10 pounds
• Large eggs	$0.61 per dozen
• Nylons	$1.00 a pair
• Ivory soap	$0.29 for 2 bars

[1] Figures taken from worldometers.info/world-population, US National Center for Health Statistics, *Divorce and Divorce Rates* US (cdc.gov/nchs/data/series/sr_21/sr21_029.pdf) and United States Census Bureau, *Historical Marital Status Tables* (census.gov/data/tables/time-series/demo/families/marital.html).
[2] Figures taken from thepeoplehistory.com.

Image Attributions

Photographs and images used in this book are reproduced courtesy of the following:

Page 4 – Advertisement from *Life* Magazine, 1st Aug 1955. Source: books.google.com/books?id=xlYEAAAAMBAJ&printsec. Pre 1978, no copyright mark (PD* image).
Page 6 – Image cropped from Mutual of New York advertisement printed in *Life* magazine 7th Mar 1955. Source: books.google.com/books?id=JFQEAAAAMBAJ&printsec. Pre 1978, no copyright mark (PD* image).
Page 7 – Source: ushistoryscene.com/article/levittown/. Pre 1978, no copyright mark (PD* image).
Page 8 – Advertisement source: ebay.com. Pre 1978, no copyright mark (PD* image).
Page 9 – Advertisement from *Life* magazine, 7th Mar 1955. Source: books.google.com/books?id=JFQEAAAAMBAJ&printsec. Pre 1978, no copyright mark (PD* image).
Page 10 – Leadenhall Street from Bishopsgate, 1955. Creative Commons license. Photo by Ben Brooksbank.
Page 11 – Private image, unknown creator. Pre 1978, no copyright mark (PD* image).
Page 12 – Advertisement from *Life* magazine, 7th Mar 1955. Source: books.google.com/books?id=JFQEAAAAMBAJ&printsec. Pre 1978, no copyright mark (PD* image).
Page 13 – Source: flickr.com/photos/aussiefordadverts/5205760405/. Attribution-NoDerivatives 4.0 International (CC BY-ND 4.0).
Page 14 – General Motors carpark, source: books.google.com./books?id=r1YEAAAAMBAJ&printsec. Pre 1978, no copyright renewal (PD image).
Page 15 – Imperial by Chrysler, *Life* magazine, 25th July 1955. Source: books.google.com/books?id=wlYEAAAAMBAJ& printsec. – Studebaker advertisement, *Life* magazine, 14th Mar 1955. Source: books.google.com/books?id=A1QEAAAAMBAJ &printsec. – Mercury by Ford advertisement, *Life* magazine, 21st Feb 1955. Source: books.google.com/books?id= LFQEAAAAMBAJ&printsec. All images this page pre 1978, no copyright mark (PD* image).
Page 16 – MG MGA, 1955-56. Source: flickr.com/photos/andreboeni/40154877544/. – SAAB 93, 1955. Source: flickr.com/ photos/andreboeni/33663136616/. – Pegaso Z-103, 1955. Source: flickr.com/photos/andreboeni/28097457979/. All photos Attribution 4.0 International (CC BY 4.0). – Chevrolet Assembly line, 1955. This image is the property of General Motors, printed here under fair use terms for information only, as it is significant to the article created. It is rendered in low resolution to avoid piracy. It is believed that this will not in any way limit the ability of the copyright owners to market or sell the product.
Page 17 – Advertisement from *Life* magazine, 28th Feb 1955. Source: books.google.com/books?id=QIQEAAAAMBAJ&printsec. Pre 1978, no copyright mark (PD* image).
Page 18 – Advertisement from *Life* magazine, 7th Mar 1965. Source: books.google.com/books?id=JFQEAAAAMBAJ&printsec. Pre 1978, no copyright mark (PD* image).
Page 19 – 50s family, source: flickr.com/photos/brizzlebornandbred/23023833354. Attribution 4.0 (Creative Commons (CC) BY 4.0). – *Warner Brothers Presents*, 1955 by Warner Brothers. Source: imdb.com/title/tt0047786/mediaviewer/ rm3026790144. This image is the property of Warner Brothers, printed here under fair use terms for information only, as it is significant to the article created. It is rendered in low resolution to avoid piracy. It is believed that this will not in any way limit the ability of the copyright owners to market or sell their product.
Page 20 – *The $64,000 Question*, 1955 by CBS Television. This image is the property of CBS, printed here under fair use terms for information only, as it is significant to the article created. It is rendered in low resolution to avoid piracy. It is believed that this will not in any way limit the ability of the copyright owners to market or sell their product. – *General Electric Theatre*, 1955 by CBS Television. Source: en.wikipedia.org/wiki/General_Electric_Theater. Pre 1978, no copyright mark (PD image).
Page 21 – *The Millionaire*, 8th July 1957, by CBS Television. Source: commons.wikimedia.org/wiki/File: Angie_Dickenson_ James_Craig_The_Millionaire_1957.JPG. Pre 1978, no copyright mark (PD image). – The original Mouseketeers from the first week of *The Mickey Mouse Club*, 3rd Oct 1955. This image is the property of Disney, printed here under fair use terms for information only, as it is significant to the article created. It is rendered in low resolution to avoid piracy. It is believed that this will not in any way limit the ability of the copyright owners to market or sell their product. – *Gunsmoke* circa 1955, by CBS Television. Source: imdb.com/title/tt0047736/mediaviewer/rm929144065. Pre 1978, (PD image). – *The Adventures of Robin Hood* by Sapphire Films. This image is the property of Sapphire Films, printed here under fair use terms for information only, as it is significant to the article created. It is rendered in low resolution to avoid piracy and should not in any way limit the ability of the copyright owners to sell their product.
Page 22 – Source: americanhistory.si.edu/blog/2011/10/food-culture.html. Pre 1978, no copyright mark (PD image).
Page 23 – MacDonalds, creators unknown. Pre 1978, no copyright mark (PD image).
Page 24 – Source: dailymail.co.uk/femail/article-5249797/Adverts-1940s-50s-60s-world-changed. Pre 1978, (PD image).
Page 25 – Rosa Parks with Dr. King printed in *Ebony* Magazine, 1955. Source: en.wikipedia.org/wiki/Rosa_Parks from United States Information Agency (Bureau of Public Affairs). Pre 1978, no copyright mark (PD image). – Parks riding a bus, 21st Dec 1965, source: loc.gov/pictures/item/94505572/ from the Library of Congress, (PD image). – Parks fingerprinted by Lieutenant D.H. Lackey, 22nd Feb 1956 (PD image). – Bus 2857, source: en.wikipedia.org/wiki/Rosa_Parks. CC BY-SA 3.0. – Parks statue in the National Civil Rights Museum, Memphis, TN. Source: commons.wikimedia.org/wiki/File:Rosa_parks_ human_rights_museum_memphis_2.jpg. CC Attribution-Share Alike 4.0 International. – Parks statue at US Capitol by Eugene Daub, 2013. Source: aoc.gov/explore-capitol-campus/art/rosa-parks. (PD image).
Page 26 – Missile launch, this image is the work of the U.S. federal government. Pre 1978, no mark (PD image).
Page 27 – CIDG unit training. Source: pbs.org/kenburns/the-vietnam-war/episodes/and en.wikipedia.org/wiki/Civilian_ Irregular_Defense_Group_program. This image is the work of the U.S. federal government. Pre 1978, no mark (PD image).
Page 28 – Advertisement from *Life* Magazine, 7th Feb 1955. Source: books.google.com/books?id=6VMEAAAAMBAJ& printsec. Pre 1978, no copyright mark (PD* image).
Page 29 – Poster images from BOAC and BEA, 1955. Copyright for film poster art is most likely owned by either the publisher or the creator of the work. These posters are for information only and are reproduced under fair use terms. The images are rendered in low resolution to avoid piracy. It is believed these images will not in any way limit the ability of the copyright owner to sell their product. Pre 1978, no copyright mark (PD* image).
Page 30 – *The Daily Princetonian* extra edition released 18th Apr 1955. Pre 1978, no copyright mark (PD image). – Einstein in 1947 from the United States Library of Congress Prints and Photographs division digital ID cph.3b46036, source: commons.wikimedia.org/wiki/File:Albert_Einstein_Head.jpg. (PD image).
Page 31 – Juan Perón, source: en.wikipedia.org/wiki/Juan_Perón#/media/File:Juan_Perón_1946.jpg. (PD image). – Eva Perón, source: commons.wikimedia.org/wiki/File:Evita_con_traje_formal.jpg. (PD image).
Page 32 – Novak and Stewart, 1958. Source: commons.wikimedia.org/wiki/File:Kim_Novak_James_Stewart_Vertigo_ Still.jpg by Paramount Pictures. Pre 1978, no copyright mark (PD image). – Newman studio publicity still, en.wikipedia.org/wiki/Paul_Newman#/media/File:Paul_Newman_1954.JPG. Pre 1978, no copyright mark (PD image). – Eastwood, creator unknown, circa 1955. Source: reddit.com/r/OldSchoolCool/comments/fnkucq/a_dashing_young_ clint_eastwood_1955/ by u/langator. Pre 1978 (PD image).
Page 33 – Marilyn Monroe publicity photo for *The Seven Year Itch*, 1955 by Twentieth Century-Fox. Source: en.wikipedia.org/wiki/The_Seven_Year_Itch#/media/File:Marilyn_Monroe_photo_pose_Seven_Year_Itch.jpg. (PD image). – *Guys and Dolls* poster, 1955, by MGM. Source: famousfix.com/topic/guys-and-dolls. – *Lady and the Tramp* movie poster, 1955, by Disney. Source: posteritati.com/poster/47783/lady-and-the-tramp-1955-us-herald. Copyright for film poster art is most likely owned by either the publisher or the creator of the work. These posters are for information only and are reproduced under fair use terms. The images are rendered in low resolution to avoid piracy. It is believed these images will not in any way limit the ability of the copyright owner to sell their product. Pre 1978, no copyright mark (PD* image).
Page 34 – Advertisement from *Life* Magazine, 28th Feb 1955. Source: books.google.com/books?id=QIQEAAAAMBAJ&printsec. Pre 1978, no copyright mark (PD* image).

Page 35 – Theatre poster, 1955. Source: wnyc.org/story/cat-on-a-hot-tin-roof/. Pre 1978, no copyright mark (PD image). – Stage and film montage, source: broadway.com/buzz/166691/cats-meow-how-tennessee-williams-cat-on-a-hot-tin-roof-keeps-prowling-back-to-broadway/. – Movie poster, 1958, by MGM. Source: en.wikipedia.org/wiki/Cat_on_a_Hot_Tin_Roof_(1958_film). Copyright not renewed (PD image).

Page 36 – James Dean, source: needpix.com/photo/222883. Pre 1978, no copyright mark (PD image). – Dean in his Spyder, and news footage of the crash site. Source: wikimapia.org/2254780/James-Dean-s-fatal-car-accident-actual-site. Images are included here for information only under U.S. fair use laws due to: 1- No free alternative exists of the event; 2- images are low resolution copies; 3- these do not limit the copyright owner's rights to sell the products in any way; 4- Copies are too small to be used to make illegal copies for another book; 5- The images are significant to the article created.

Page 37 – James Dean in *East of Eden* and *Rebel Without a Cause*, 1955, by Warner Bros. Source: en.wikipedia.org/wiki/James_Dean. (PD images). – In *Giant*, 1956, by Warner Bros. Source: flickr.com/photos/elizafairy/3683651704. Attribution 4.0 International (CC BY 4.0).

Page 38 – Source: vintageadbrowser.com/photography-ads-1950s/9. Pre 1978, no copyright renewal (PD image).

Page 39 – Source: jana-treeclimber.blogspot.com/2012/09/. Pre 1978, no copyright renewal (PD image).

Page 40 – Family at Disneyland, Anaheim, California, 1956. Source: flickr.com/photos/iisg/4586688368/. Attribution-ShareAlike 4.0 International (CC BY-SA 4.0). – Original Mickey and Donald, 17th July 1955. Source: flickr.com/photos/iisg/4586688368. Attribution-ShareAlike 4.0 International (CC BY-SA 4.0). – Walt Disney, 17th July 1955. Source: thisdayin disneyhistory.com/DisneylandGrandOpening.html. Creator unknown, no copyright mark (PD image). – Ronald Regan, screen still from *Dateline: Disneyland* on ABC. Source: yesterland.com/dl1955.html. Screen still reproduced here under terms of Fair Use. The image is not replaceable by free content. The image is scaled-down and low-resolution to avoid piracy. It is believed that the image will not in any way limit the ability of the copyright owners to sell their product.

Page 41 – Advertisement from *Life* Magazine, 14th Feb 1955. Source: books.google.com/books?id=N1QEAAAAMBAJ &printsec. Pre 1978, no copyright mark (PD* image).

Page 42 – *Lord of the Rings* books, source: abebooks.com/rare-books/most-expensive-sales/year-2015.shtml?cm_sp. Pre 1978, no copyright mark (PD image). – *Lord of the Rings* movie posters, 2001-2003, by New Line Cinema. Copyright for film poster art is most likely owned by either the publisher or the creator of the work. All posters reproduced here under terms of Fair Use. The images are not replaceable by free content. The images used are scaled-down, low-resolution images to avoid piracy. It is believed that these images will not in any way limit the ability of the copyright owners to sell their product.

Page 43 – Images courtesy of guinnessworldrecords.com. These images are for information only, are significant to the article and are reproduced under fair use terms. The images are rendered in low resolution to avoid piracy. It is believed these images will not in any way limit the ability of the copyright owners to market or sell their product.

Page 44 – Bell magazine advertisement, 1950s. Source unknown. Pre 1978, no copyright renewal (PD image).

Page 45 – Lewis, source: en.wikipedia.org/wiki/Jerry_Lee_Lewis. Pre 1978, no copyright mark (PD image). – Haley, source: en.wikipedia.org/wiki/Bill_Haley_%26_His_Comets. Pre 1978, no copyright mark (PD image). – Sun Records, source: commons.wikimedia.org/wiki/File:Sun_Studio_Memphis.jpg. Pre 1978, no copyright mark (PD image).

Page 46 – Prado, source: granma.cu/cultura/2017-11-17/mambo-que-rico-es-17-11-2017-22-11-42 creator unknown. Pre 1978 (PD image). – Haley, sheet music cover image from *Rock Around the Clock*, Decca Records. Source: wikiwand.com/en/Rock_Around_the_Clock. Pre 1978 (PD image). – Boone, source: en.wikipedia.org/wiki/Pat_Boone. Pre 1978 (PD image). – Gibbs, record cover of *Dance With Me Henry* for Modern Records 1955. Pre 1978, no copyright renewal (PD image).

Page 47 – Sinatra by Columbia Pictures 1957, source: en.wikipedia.org/wiki/Frank_Sinatra. Pre 1978, (PD image). – Cole publicity photo by GAC 1958, source: commons.wikimedia.org/wiki/File:Nat_King_Cole_1958.JPG. Pre 1978, (PD image).

Page 48 – Dress, 1955. Source: flickr.com/photos/30453277@N03/6526062925. Pre 1978, no copyright mark (PD image).

Page 49 – Images from myvintagevogue.com. Pre 1978, no copyright mark (PD image).

Page 50 – Dior's New Look, sketches by author. – Models wear Christian Dior, 1955. Creators unknown. Pre 1978, no copyright mark (PD image).

Page 51 – Bullet Bra advertisement, source: *British Vogue*, October 1955. Pre 1978, no copyright mark (PD* image). – Advertisement for Toni Todd dresses, source: *Charm Magazine*, January 1955. Pre 1978, no copyright mark (PD* image).

Page 52 – Advertisement from *Life* Magazine, 7th Nov 1955. Source: books.google.com/books?id=xFQEAAAAMBAJ& printsecc. Pre 1978, no copyright mark (PD* image).

Page 53 – Spiegel, source: ebay.com. Pre 1978, no copyright mark (PD image).

Page 54 – Advertisement from *Life* Magazine, 4th July 1955. Source: books.google.com/books?id=r1YEAAAAMBAJ&printsec. Pre 1978, no copyright mark (PD* image).

Page 55 – Advertisement from *Life* Magazine, 28th Mar 1955. Source: books.google.com/books?id=FlQEAAAAMBAJ& printsec. Pre 1978, no copyright mark (PD* image). – Dress patterns, source: sovintagepatterns.com/VINTAGE-PATTERNS-1950s_c_13-6-4.html. Pre 1978, no copyright mark (PD* image). – Monroe, source: commons.wikimedia.org/wiki/File: Marilyn_Monroe_at_Ciro%27s.jpg. Pre 1978, no copyright mark (PD image).

Page 56 – Sinatra, source: morrisonhotelgallery.com/collections/wtvp8g/The-Sinatra-Experience-. – Brando, source: dailybreak.co/wp-content/uploads/2019/06/Marlon-Brando-Ford-Thunderbird-1955-Est.-2444.jpg. – Dean, source: en.wikipedia.org/wiki/James_Dean. All images this page pre 1978, no copyright mark (PD image).

Page 57 – Source: blog.hola.com/hongkongblues/2017/03/rosa-ahumado. Pre 1978, no copyright mark (PD image).

Page 58 – Young girl, source: polioplace.org/history/artifacts/reluctant-poster-child. Pre 1978, no mark (PD image). – Iron Lung ward, source: commons.wikimedia.org/wiki/File:Iron_Lung_ward-Rancho_Los_Amigos_Hospital.gif by fda.gov (PD image). – Children's ward, source: imgur.com/gallery/vdwfM40. Pre 1978, no copyright mark (PD image).

Page 59 – GAM-63 RASCAL, source: commons.wikimedia.org/wiki/File:GAM-63_RASCAL_on_trailer.jpg from the U.S. Air Force (PD image). – Oklahoma! film poster, 1955 by RKO Radio Pictures. Source: en.wikipedia.org/wiki/Oklahoma!_(1955_film) (PD image).

Page 60 – Coke advertisement, source unknown. Pre 1978, no copyright mark (PD* image). – USS Nautilus (SSN 571), 21st Jan 1954, from U.S. Navy. Source: commons.wikimedia.org/wiki/File:Nautiluscore.jpg. (PD image).

Page 61 – Le Manns 1955, creator unknown. Source: carlosghys.be/html/biography_luc.html. Pre 1978, no copyright mark (PD image). – *Lolita* book cover, 1955, by Vladimir Nabokov. Pre 1978, no copyright mark (PD image). – *Lolita* movie poster, 1962, by MGM. Source: en.wikipedia.org/wiki/Lolita_(1962_film)#/media/File:Lolita_(1962_film_poster).jpg. Pre 1978 (PD image).

Page 62 – Advertisement from *Life* magazine, 7th Mar 1955. Source: books.google.com/books?id=JFQEAAAAMBAJ& printsec. Pre 1978, no copyright mark (PD* image).

Page 63 – Advertisement from *Life* magazine, 3rd Jan 1965. Source: books.google.com/books?id=_VMEAAAAMBAJ& printsec. Pre 1978, no copyright mark (PD* image).

Page 64 & 65 – All photos are, where possible, CC BY 2.0 or PD images made available by the creator for free use including commercial use. Where commercial use photos are unavailable, photos are included here for information only under U.S. fair use laws due to: 1- images are low resolution copies; 2- images do not devalue the ability of the copyright holders to profit from the original works in any way; 3- Images are too small to be used to make illegal copies for use in another book; 4- The images are relevant to the article created.

Page 66 – Advertisement from *Life* Magazine, 1st Aug 1955. Source: books.google.com/books?id=xlYEAAAAMBAJ&printsec. Pre 1978, no copyright mark (PD* image).

These words first appeared in print in the year 1955.

gangbusters

Microwave oven

counterintuitive

fabric softener

Artificial Intelligence

Big Bang Theory

certified mail

Fallout Shelter

DIY

Information Science

mind-boggling

AEROSPACE

Intensive Care Unit

home computer

SPECIAL FORCES

STRESS TEST

skydiving

* From merriam-webster.com/time-traveler/1955.

Please help me out:

I sincerely hope you enjoyed reading this book and that it brought back many fond memories from the past.

I have enjoyed researching and writing this book for you and would greatly appreciate your feedback by way of a written review and/or star rating.

First and foremost, I am always looking to grow and improve as a writer. It is reassuring to hear what works, as well as to receive constructive feedback on what could improve.

Second, starting out as an unknown author is exceedingly difficult, and Customer Reviews go a long way toward making the journey out of anonymity possible.

Please help me by taking a few moments to leave a review for others to read.

Best regards,
Bernard Bradforsand-Tyler.

Please leave a
book review/rating at:

http://bit.ly/1955reviews

Or scan the QR code:

9 780645 062328